EARTH AND SKY

Other Art Books from
New London Librarium

Selfies: (Wells Moore)

Juner's Home (Yujuan "Juner" Patnode)

Cultivating Illuminations (Mark Patnode)

Mother Goose and Other Rhymes (Sayles School Students)

Art of Love (Colleen Hennessy)

By Night or Day (Colleen Hennessy)

On Women (Colleen Hennessy)

Wheresoe'er (Colleen Hennessy)

Every Common Sight (Colleen Hennessy)

Time Gone (Lynda Wesley McLaughlin)

Earth and Sky

Nature Meditations in Word and Watercolor

Essays by Judy Benson

Illustrations by Roxanne Steed

New London Librarium

Earth & Sky: Nature Meditations in Word and Watercolor

Essays by Judy Benson
Art by Roxanne Steed
Foreword by Christine Woodside
Edited by Glenn Alan Cheney

Published by
New London Librarium
Hanover, CT 06350
NLLibrarium.com

Portions of this book were published as part of New London Landmarks' "Voices from a Pandemic" online exhibit in October 2020. "Waterfall" was published in the Connecticut Episcopal Church online newsletter in June 2020. On page 37, quote by Mary Oliver is from "Landscape," published in *Dream Work,* 1986.

ISBN: 978-1-947074-57-6

Roxanne and Judy welcome inquiries about readings, exhibits and other events. Contact them at: roxannesteed@gmail.com; moss153@att.net (Judy) and earthandskymeditations@gmail.com

To Nature

the source which fills and rescues us all,

and to everyone who cherishes and shares her wisdom and beauty.

RK Steed

Contents

Foreword

I have been lucky enough to see portions of this book while it was in the making. Here in the world of Judy and Roxanne's ramblings, melancholy mixes with joy and beauty. The novel coronavirus forced the world into a retreat, and these honest letters to the world show that even in a pandemic, a retreat opens minds to the beauty and struggle of creatures.

Judy recognizes that humans yearn for nature. She notices the smallest miracles. As a child she retreated to a secret rock in the tangle of her back yard; later her father ordered the land cleared and rock removed. Heartbreaking. In the quarantine spring of 2020, she followed a bee behind her urban community garden; it showed her a patch of wild violets. One day, watching a bird, she writes, "Me, the tree and this nuthatch—we have more in common than the same air. We are bound together in a circle of need."

Roxanne Steed's paintings bring the world of Judy's observations to life. That kind of pairing can only occur when writer and artist understand each other and explore the same ground. Some of the paintings are in journal style: she recorded her visual impressions in the field, adding notes. Some explore light and shape that natural landscapes impress upon the mind. Together, the words and paintings invite me back into the mysterious everyday and nudge me to reconnect with my deepest thoughts outdoors.

Years ago Judy and I worked in the same open newsroom at *The Day*, a New London daily. I first knew her through her writing. She'd gone to hear the author Amy Tan speak, and her story about it riveted me. I'd gone to that talk, too, but Judy had noticed something. Tan said she'd been stunned to encounter a Cliff Notes guide to *The Joy Luck Club*. The notes exaggerated Tan's personal life and suggested her book was autobiographical. Tan countered that literature is more a quilt of encounters and imagination, "the synchronicity between fluke and fiction." Tan said she had met a Chinese man stacking rocks on the beach near San Francisco; she listened to him talk about finding the proper balance and knew that unplanned encounter had to go into one of her books.

Over time I learned that Judy and I both had grown up in New Jersey with World War II generation parents. Our first explorations of the wild world occurred between lanes of crabapples, maples, and forsythia—watching birds, squirrels, skunks and bees make their way around our towns. Like Judy, I always notice that all creatures are doing their best, often with bad circumstances.

Inside the pages of this book, I imagine Judy and Roxanne wandering some water's edge, looking at rocks.

Roger Tory Peterson once said he could observe the most common sparrow for hours if the bird were cooperating. That kind of focus and respect for all creatures guides Judy's words and Roxanne's images. This volume will speak to all people, even those who think they aren't having intense experiences in nature every single day. Because everyone is.

Christine Woodside
Chester, Conn.

Preface

In this book, we share our encounters with nature through the tumultuous year of 2020. We hope our reflections will arouse your own insights. It was a strange and difficult journey we all went through collectively and individually that is worth looking back on as we move forward into an uncertain future.

Creating this book, as a dear friend pointed out, was a means of dealing with the chaos of that year. But before the writing and the painting came the time outdoors—noticing, feeling, breathing deep—the catharsis that birthed these expressions. If there's a message of hope in 2020, maybe it's that taking time out to make nature the center of attention really can help realign our perspective when we need it most.

In some of the selections, you'll find references to our faith, but that is our personal lens. We intend this as a book for people of any religion or no religion who connect with the inherent spirituality of nature.

Over the dozen years we've been friends, we've worked on several art and writing projects together, daring to hope it would one day lead to a book. We are grateful and humbled to see it come to fruition. But this is still a work in progress, with the next step in your hands.

We encourage you to read the book one selection at a time over the course of a year. Our fervent desire is that this inspires you to spend your own quiet time with the bullfrogs, the waterfalls and the wind, and gives you a focus for reflection. Then open a journal or sketchbook and fill it with your own voice and vision.

Thank you for taking this journey with us.

Peace and love,

Judy Benson
Roxanne Steed

Introduction

Earth and Sky

Lyrics of an old hymn titled "Many and Great" broke into my consciousness one morning, after a decades-long slumber in a quiet chamber of memory. Funny how that happens sometimes – a song you learned and loved as a child, all but forgotten, is suddenly and inexplicably resurrected to the tip of your tongue. Someone once told me that whenever that happens, be sure to pay attention. Your subconscious (or call it the Holy Spirit, the life force, the great mystery or any other name you prefer) may be trying to tell you something important.

This short hymn, its deep message conveyed with simple words, is set to a traditional melody of the Native American Dakota tribe. Joseph Renville, the son of a tribal member and a Canadian fur trapper, wrote the song in the 1840s, and now it resides in hymnals of many Christian denominations, my own Episcopal church among them. I remember singing it when I was 8 or 10 years old, as one of the boys in the choir proudly drummed the hiking-pace rhythm on a tom-tom: stride, step-step, stride, step-step, stride....

Many and great,
O God are thy works,
Maker of earth and sky
Thy hands have set
The heavens with stars
Thy fingers spread
the mountains and plains.
Lo, at thy word, the waters were formed
Deep seas obeyed thy voice.

Grant unto us communion with thee,
Thou star-abiding one
Come unto us,
and dwell with us,
With thee are found
the gifts of life.
Bless us with life that has no end
Eternal life with thee.

Why had I suddenly been reunited with this old, melodious friend? About a week before, I had spent a weekend at the Incarnation Center in Deep River with my dear friend Roxanne Steed, to begin a creative project we'd been talking about for a while. She would paint watercolor landscapes that would pair with my essays. These would combine in a book of reflections on nature and spirituality intended to invite people to spend time with Earth, sky and a meditative mind, and to love it all. Perhaps my recent experience walking and writing in the winter woods had, in some way, unearthed "Many and Great" as the theme song for the long unspoken urge that birthed this project. That urge was to help others connect with nature and that creative force that is within all of us and infinitely beyond us. Called God and so many other names, it's that universal essence outside the confines of human power, human understanding and the overstimulated, hyper-distracted modern world.

Earth and Sky

WINTER

Rocks

Needle Ice

Sunrise

Cedar Swamp

Shadows

Rocks tell stories to those who listen. Geologists will recount tales of rock cycles. Instead of static inert masses, they talk of rocks transforming over millennia under forces of heat, pressure, earthquakes and volcanoes. These give birth to the congregations of minerals compacted into giant masses, only to be moved, weathered by the elements and transported by wind and water as pebbles, stones of all sizes and tiny shards—raw materials for soil and the beginnings of the next rock cycle.

In the landscape of the Northeast, rocks left by the glaciers dominate many forests and coastal inlets. Hikers may have a favorite boulder—one split by a lightning strike or holding a miniature forest garden of ferns that naturalists call a polypody or offering a lookout above the waves on the rocky shore. But the permanence that human admirers ascribe to them is an illusion. The rocks are changing imperceptibly through the erosion and persistence of moss, lichen and the elements. A sudden storm and rising seas may suddenly lift what seemed immovable.

My favorite rock is from my childhood. It exists no more—at least not in the form that I knew it. Made from the common gray granite of so many of its glacial kin there in northern New Jersey and the rest of the Northeast, it had a sloped front I would try to slide down, despite the bumpy surface. A wide crack down the front had filled with a velvet ribbon of moss, making a vibrant green stripe set off against the dark stone. It had a flat top that made a throne where I could pretend to be a queen. Sitting there, I was the benevolent ruler of the little forest in my backyard, of the mighty oaks, the rhododendron that made a canopy bed inside its branches, of the squirrels and the robins and earthworms. When I and my neighborhood friends Lee Ann and Leona were looking for something to do, we often ended up in this quarter-acre woodland, gathering sticks for make-believe fires, catching bugs, mixing mud pies to dry in the sun on stone ovens.

This pocket of nature existed amidst a neighborhood of small lots and older houses, duplexes and apartments. The home I grew up in had a small front yard and a typically sized back lawn. But through some fluke of how the street was divided into private properties, our back yard adjoined an undeveloped lot left wild. The wild lot came with the rest of the property when my parents bought it, and they left it alone for my first 10 years or so. Then one day, for reasons I never understood, my father hired landscapers to turn the back lot into lawn with a bulldozer, chain saws and truck to haul away the giant boulders. My favorite rock disappeared. By then I was too old for playing queen, but I missed my rock and the shady palace where it was the finest furniture.

Once, as part of a writing workshop, I was asked to consider my childhood landscape as the frame of reference for my relationship with nature. As I considered the assignment, I went back to that New Jersey neighborhood generally, but more specifically to that back lot woodland and even precisely to that favorite rock. I imagined myself sitting atop it, my bare summer legs enjoying the cool stone, birds chirping in the trees above. It was, I now realize, the place I first loved nature and it seemed to love me back. This was, I believe, how I first experienced God's love for me and all of creation. If I could have articulated it then, I would have told my father the rock was sacred.

I'm glad I at least had that time before the bulldozers to get to know that piece of nature. It was the foundation of a lifelong love of the outdoors and how it could touch my soul. Reflecting back on the destruction of that wild place still makes me sad, but also renews my conviction that we need to give others the chance to fall in love with nature and let themselves feel loved in return.

Needle Ice

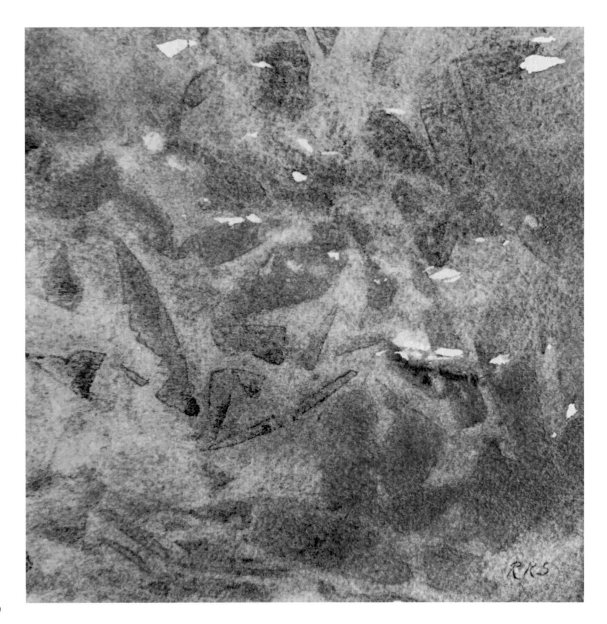

One of the joys and challenges of trekking through the woods is the necessity of looking around—all around. Even in a nearly snowless winter, when the trees are bare and the understory is mostly shades of gray and brown, there are wonders to discover in the morning sun piercing through the open canopy, shapely arms of trees against the vivid blue sky, glowing green moss and crystal castles at your feet. But only if you take the 360-degree view.

Today's obsessive attention to screens large and small can almost make that behavior seem quaint and unnecessary. But it's not, if enjoying nature to its fullest is your aim. If you set out looking for beauty and wonder in nature, you will find it, and your spirit will be better equipped for the paradox of being human, capable of great love and great cruelty, so often stuck in pain yet still reaching for something higher.

Hiking with my friend Roxanne on a clear, cold February morning, we took in all the marvels of creation in our midst at this woodland retreat center. The end of the hike led us on a trail beside a lake where campers swim, fish and canoe in the summer. In the exposed soil next to the trail, we noticed clusters of strange white rods, about the size of sewing needles, poking upright out of the earth. Looking closer, we saw these were bundles of tiny icicles. In their geometric array atop the ground, the icicles resembled a crystal palace from a fairy story.

Neither of us had ever noticed this before. We later learned these formations are called needle ice. It happens in mild winters, without the prolonged frigid spell needed for the ground to freeze. On those days when the air temperature dips below 32 degrees, yet the ground stays warmer, places like this on the downward slope to the lake are prime spots for needle ice. Groundwater below the surface is pushed up by capillary action, and freezes in these needle shapes when it reaches the air. These delicate, glasslike and ephemeral jewels of the trail seemed to me like softly glowing beacons, summoning us to look outside ourselves and be part of nature's great pageant even for a moment by getting close, looking up, down and all around.

Golden veil unfurling upward on the horizon, sunrise on this February morning came just before 7 a.m., then lifted gently behind the naked winter woods. Within 20 minutes or so, the intense yellows, oranges, reds and purples that painted the sky disappeared, the sun now high in the pale blue sky.

Witnessing a winter sunrise is a rare occurrence for me, as it must be for many others. Daily lives of work and family responsibilities filled with distractions leave little chance for the stillness required to be present for this free offering grace from the Earth. Yet it is always there, waiting for us.

After the sunrise, I started getting ready for the day. But not before more window-gazing. A chipmunk appeared on the mossy earth outside, darting to and fro then stopping on a rock, perhaps for his own brief experience of stillness. Did our eyes meet through the glass? I think so. No matter, the encounter from my side was enough to remind me that sharing this space with other creatures is a privilege to treasure and protect, in whatever ways we can. Just appreciating it and encouraging others to do the same is one of the simplest yet most powerful.

Cedar Swamp

24

Atlantic white cedars create their own islands. The roots of these storied evergreens, once highly sought after for shipbuilding, course everywhere through the watery pools of the swamp. The roots clustered at the base of the tree capture sediments and fallen needles that fill in the spaces to form little islands. It's a distinct part of the personality of the cedar swamp. The roots stand out as vividly as the trees themselves.

To venture into one of these now rare habitats feels like something primeval, where dinosaurs and tree-sized ferns wouldn't seem out of place. That's especially true in winter. The gray-brown mosaic of the dormant hardwood forest turns suddenly into a different world where the dirt trail becomes a boardwalk through the swamp. Here, every rock, root and log is covered with bright green moss or mint green fungus. This green glow sets off black pools topped with geometric patterns of ice. Most of the sky is obscured by the deep green crowns of cedars. Passing through the swamp is like being inside the envelope of a parallel sphere, with some thin, invisible curtain around it.

Atlantic white cedar swamps have never been common, existing only along a narrow band 20 or so miles inland from the coast. Lumbering and development destroyed many, leaving only scattered examples preserved by public parks and conservation groups. Was their effort worthwhile? Should they have just given up, deciding that the economic forces were just too strong?

Let's be thankful those healers of the Earth kept going, not giving in to doubts. Like the cedars, their roots stand out—roots of love for nature and for people. What if we all started seeing ourselves as healers of the Earth?

Shadows on a bright morning in the winter woods defy the stereotype. Instead of looking gloomy or oppressive, shadows of spreading branches, leafless limbs and skyward-reaching trunks across the trail emphasize their presence, their prominence. Trees are in charge here, they seem to say. Pay attention to them.

When the winter sun rises in a cloudless sky after a snowfall, the crisscrossing shadows of trees and shrubs make the snow crystals sparkle clearer. The chiaroscuro effect of black against white tickles the pupils. It can be almost blinding.

But shadows have another side, too. They can make something benign look eerie in the way they reveal and sometimes exaggerate shapes. Things can hide in the shadows, or get lost in them. Though the silhouettes created when something blocks the light aren't a tangible thing, they can possess a strange power over another creature's perception and action.

Here in the winter woods, trees and their long shadows make a place for passing humans to cultivate humility. Who could not be humbled and grateful to be enveloped by the beautiful weave of branches overhead and shadows below?

Spring

Whitecaps

Perch

White Violets

Moss

Shadbush

Dirt Road

Whitecaps

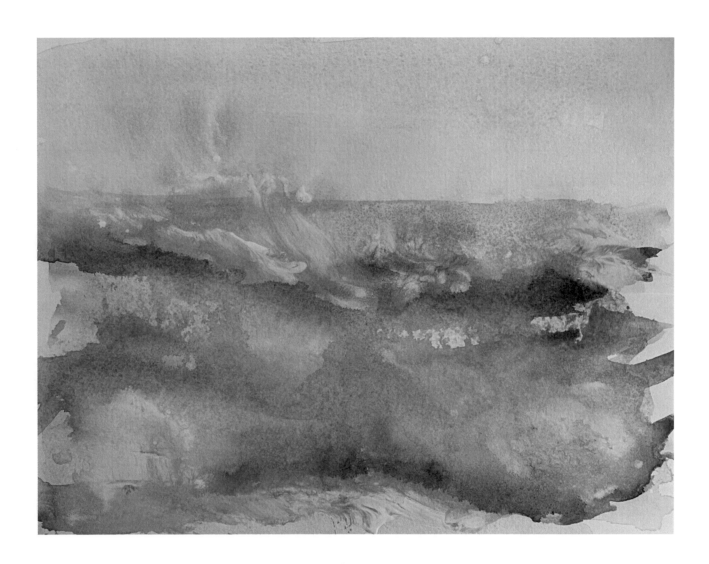

Winds whipped the silvery green seas into whitecaps as a flock of brants paddled figure eights around rocks just offshore. When these common seabirds caught a wave just right, they could body surf with the lightness of children frolicking at the beach.

The whitecaps looked playful, too, like foamy balls of energy rising out of the depths to tickle the breeze before ducking back under. Nature offered these scenes as free gifts to anyone who paused to receive. I was grateful to be in the right mindset to welcome them this particular morning in this particular place, and hoped the other people spread across this public landscape were experiencing it, too, especially in this strange world we were now dwelling in.

I had walked three miles from my home that morning to Harkness Memorial State Park, a former farm and estate with expansive lawns, treasured flower gardens, natural marsh and a horseshoe-shaped shoreline on Long Island Sound that is half sandy, half rocky. It was the Saturday before Easter at the height of the global coronavirus pandemic, when most of us had been spending most of every day staying home and away from others. Weary of too much time on the computer, I craved time in open spaces, amid sun, clouds, wind and chirping birds. Thankfully, this park remained a place where enjoying the outdoors while keeping a safe distance was still possible.

On my way to the park, an older friend from church pulled up in her car next to me. As I chatted with her through my homemade face mask about how she was doing, and she told me someone in her apartment building was sick with the virus. "That must be worrisome," I offered, wishing I could say something more reassuring. She said she was heading to Harkness, too.

The rest of the way to the park took me past neighborhoods of large houses with sweeping lawns, smaller homes with compact yards, and condominiums with shared green spaces. Interspersed between were swampy woodland patches where broad green fans of skunk cabbage carpeted the floor. Though trying to give all my attention to whatever nature I found along the way, I couldn't help feeling preoccupied. Did my friend have a face mask? If I saw her at the park, I would offer her mine to take home and wash, and make myself another.

At the park, I wandered through the newly awakened gardens and then towards the path beside the rocky shore where I spotted my friend. I waved, and walked just close enough to talk. She told me she had a mask, so she didn't need mine. For two weeks she had stayed away from her job at a nearby store because, she said, at her age she is too vulnerable. "That was a good decision," I told her. She nodded and smiled. We told each other to stay safe. Onward along the path she went, while I headed across the rocks to get closer to the whitecaps I saw dancing offshore.

Neither of us knew then when or how this bizarre episode would end. The pandemic had altered so much already, and surely some of the changes wouldn't just be temporary. But no matter what happened, we would be okay, as long as we knew how to keep our hearts open to nature and to the simple gifts of caring for one another.

Perch

Easter morning the chorus that proclaimed the joy of life came from the treetops, not the choir loft inside the sanctuary. Before the online service that morning, while the pandemic kept churches and so many other places closed, I took a short walk to where my street dead-ends in a wooded wetland. As I approached, the montage of bird music greeting me sounded like it could have inspired Aaron Copland to write a sequel to *Appalachian Spring*. It invited my spirit along with my gaze upwards.

From there I heard long clear tones and short sharp chirps, and the low rat-a-tat of two woodpeckers, all at once. I looked for the source of one close call and spotted a nuthatch on a high perch close to the edge. From this perch the nuthatch surveyed the little piece of the world we shared for a brief few moments.

What is it like to be a nuthatch, or the tree that offers its limbs as a place to rest? My own fingers have been a perch for a pet cockatiel, and my arm for a trained parrot at the zoo. Me, the tree and this nuthatch—we have more in common than the same air. We are bound together in a circle of need. I need the beauty and fresh air of trees and birdsong. The nuthatch needs a perch to rest and look out for a partner, food and predators. The tree needs me to care about them both.

34

Ragged with last season's kale and dandelions squatting in the beds, the community garden had nonetheless started to return to life by mid-April. I and some of the other gardeners already had peas and spinach rising in our plots. Pandemic restrictions had altered routines here, too—group work day would be postponed, no children would be allowed to visit. Wearing gloves to open the gate was requested.

I went to check on my beds and plant a few more radishes and turnip seeds. Sue, another gardener, was there, but she left soon after I arrived. "Hope you and your family stay safe," she said. "You, too," I answered.

I planted my seeds and decided to linger. The vibe of this time of social isolation and staying home seems all about stepping back, taking things in. I sat at one of the picnic tables until a fat bumble bee caught my eye. His soft buzz filled my ear. What was it looking for? I got up and followed. It flitted over countless weeds, meandering in spirals and curls, then would disappear under cover of leaves close to the ground. In a few seconds, back out it would fly to resume wandering. It found its way into a crevice at a corner of one of the garden beds, but stayed only for a blink.

My eyes kept following. My five-year-old self seemed to be reemerging. Then my tiny guide met up with another bumble bee. I lost track of the first and let the second lead the way. It took me to a small patch of white violets. I hadn't noticed it before. Diminutive wild cousins of domesticated pansies, purple and white violets are just one of nature's many riches, popping up in yards and wooded areas with no human effort. The deep purple ones are lovely, but the white ones—tinged with purple streaks—are the rarer, more precious beauties. A bumble bee showed them to me. That's what can come from slowing down long enough to stay curious about another creature's reality.

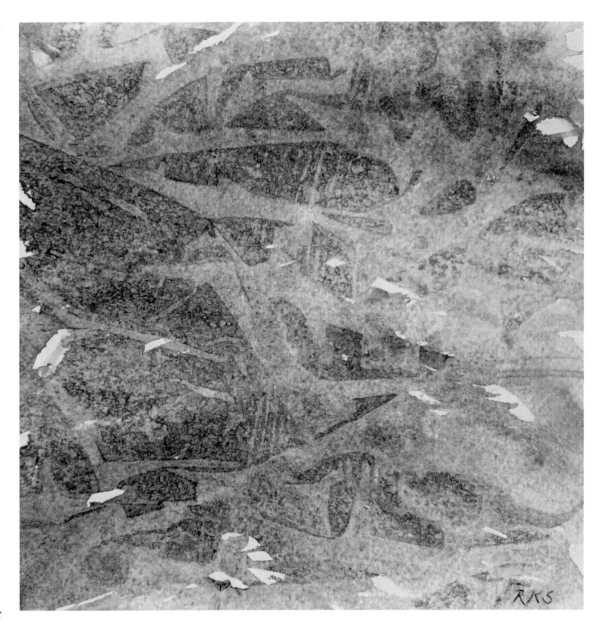

Moss

36

Spring came like no other. The blooming daffodils, clucking wood frogs and warming soil shouted "life" as I and my fellow two-legged animals who usually act like we own the planet wandered by under a haze of melancholy. Or so it seemed some days as the weeks of pandemic lockdown dragged on.

But giving in to malaise wouldn't get me or any of us through this. When I awoke the next morning to birdsong and bright sun, I knew some miles of walking would set me right. So I set off, stopping to fondle fuzzy-headed fiddleheads and maples festooned with green flowers and listen to the song of the little twisting stream gurgling towards the sea. Thoughts of the virus were never far—my face mask hung around my neck, at the ready should someone approach. But nature offered a salve.

A fallen tree just off the path caught my eye. It had once been a giant in this young forest of saplings, at least 20 feet tall and 2½ feet in diameter. But its years of reaching skyward had ended, and now it lay on the forest floor, incubating new life. Beetles and grubs made nests in the rotting wood, now fraying to nourish a new generation of woodland life. A carpet of moss in shades from chartreuse to olive green spread along the top of the log, doing its meticulous best to grow and transform—or transform to grow as it softens the bark beneath it. Moss makes its home on diverse mediums—bare soil, stream banks, atop submerged stones—greening up the hardest places with its soft persistence. On another recent walk, a large boulder furred with thick neon-green moss caught my eye, as the early afternoon sunlight cast its fire on the surface. I recalled a favorite line from a Mary Oliver poem, one that stuns me with truth no matter how often I read it:

"Isn't it plain that the sheets of moss, except that they have no tongues, could lecture all day if they wanted about spiritual patience?"

Fragments of that boulder were feeding the earth with minerals released under the touch of moss, a process happening at scales hardly comprehensible to human minds. The moss-covered log would succumb, too. As day gives way to night and night to day, death and life, breakdown and rebirth flow in endless spirals that the fiddlehead ferns reference. Being reminded of nature's way brought me comfort, seeming more familiar than the alien world of human life in a pandemic.

Later, back home after my long amble, I got news that a friend, her husband and two young children had all fallen ill with coronavirus. I grew heartsick with worry, and a sleepless night followed. But fretting wouldn't help them, so the next day I put together a care package of colored pencils, coloring books and a game, ordered a food basket sent to their house and prepared to deliver meals later in the week. My friend sent her thanks and gratitude in text messages and photos of the colored pictures. She said she loved me. I love you, I replied. They were the only words for this moment. By the end of that week, her and her family's symptoms had lessened. Fears of the worst ebbed.

I thought again of the moss. I remembered the Sanskrit writings that are the foundation of yoga, where green represents the energy of the heart, of love and transformation. Moss grows with a green fire that really does soften the hardest places. Love does too—love given, love received, love acknowledged.

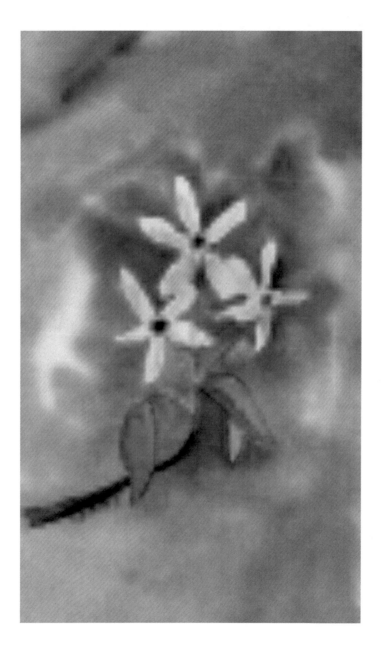

Shadbush

Star-shaped blossoms cluster at the tips of the thin branches, seeming almost to hang in midair. The white flowers of the shadbush, fully opened as shad swim from marine waters into freshwater streams to spawn, announce the coming of spring's fullness in the forest, even as the yolk-colored trout lilies and marsh marigolds pop from the dark earth below. With leggy limbs spread wide apart for plenty of sky between them, shadbush color and feed the forest through the seasons. The flowers turn into blue-black berries edible by birds and people alike. Native to these Northeast woods, shadbush recall connections that transcend time and space —interior forests to oceans, people to fish that sustained them.

Native Americans watched for the blossoms to know when to head to the rivers to net shad. Colonists adopted the habit, both to start fishing and to know when the ground had thawed enough to bury those who had died over the winter. That accounts for its other common name, serviceberry.

Shad sustained troops who nearly starved at Valley Forge during the Revolution. Decades later, industrial-scale shad fishing nearly wiped them out altogether, before common sense and restraint intervened. Today, they endure.

Shadbush, too, endures. As its gangly arms wave freely in soft spring breezes, it sends out reminders of history and how people once read nature's signs. We still can.

Dirt Road

Hard packed by countless footsteps, stroller wheels, bicycle tires and occasional horse hoofs, the way most go at Bluff Point State Park is really more of a dirt road than a woodland trail. This late May morning, the parking lot is already half full by 8, as this refuge for flora and fauna draws the weary in droves through the days of lockdown.

With the walkers and bikers came reminders of the pandemic, even as the worse of the crisis began to ease. Some hiked up face masks when passing others, and a few lost masks lay along the road. Still, bird song, briny air off the water and the mosaic of sun and shade through the trees enveloped the atmosphere. Human troubles persist, but places for respite and renewal do, too.

The road here passes a succession of hardwood forest, tidal coves, marshes, cobbled beaches and rocky promontory where the view spans to open sea, surf and soaring gulls. The varied landscape keeps even easily bored travelers refreshed along this three-mile loop. This is nature at its most accessible to seasoned wilderness hikers and infrequent outdoorsmen alike, with a wide open corridor free of anxiety for those prone to getting lost in the woods.

Honeysuckle blossoms scented the air that day, and buttercup flowers glowed in the sun. Just off the trail, a cluster of buttercups brightened the top of the 300-year-old remains of the cut stone foundation of Gov. John Winthrop Jr.'s house. Nearby, honeysuckle colonized a crevice in a large boulder called Sunset Rock. Nature doesn't have to be far away or hard to reach or unusual to feed our need to connect with the reality beyond human life.

Many side paths wander off this well-worn way, made by bicycles and boots seeking more secluded spots to meander. Still, the main road tells the main story. A placed so deeply traversed, under human power of feet or bicycle, must be speaking to some common hunger. Across the many divides in our species, we can still share a dirt road to rediscover ourselves in nature.

Summer

Bullfrogs

Waterfall

Beach

Starlight

Shelter

Bullfrogs

Environmental racism is one of those mouthful-of-sawdust sounding terms that unwittingly turns visceral pain into an academic abstraction. It's the umbrella phrase for all the ways that black and brown people in this country and the world suffer far more of the physical and mental health damage wrought by polluted land, water, air and toxic exposure from unsafe housing, workplaces and neighborhoods. Climate change has already damaged the lives of communities of color most profoundly, and that will only intensify unless bold and decisive action starts soon. If you're a person who cares about the environment, racism is your issue, too.

In early June, just as the worst of the pandemic began to ease in the Northeast, we collectively witnessed the horror of George Floyd's killing, and the response that coalesced into powerful protests in communities large and small. My husband Tom and I joined one of the throngs, a youth-led march through the main thoroughfare of Groton where we shouted "Black Lives Matter" and "No Justice, No Peace, No Racist Police" through our face masks. Worries about the virus lingered, but being silent in this moment felt just as risky.

Back home in New London after the march, I sought out the bullfrogs. They lived in a small pond in Mitchell Woods, a shady oasis in the city owned by Mitchell College. For the past couple of weeks I'd been a frequent visitor, spreading the word to my friends and neighbors about the magnificent frog chorus performing there several times a day. Sometimes as I first approached the pond, all I would hear were scattered gulps and splashes, but often if I waited they would start their song. Sometimes the singing would already be in full-throated crescendo when I arrived.

Croaking isn't the right word to describe their sound. That implies something akin to a burp—crude and involuntary (if effective at inspiring human humility). The bullfrogs vocalized with rhythm and intention, starting with one voice building into something that sounds like an orchestra of tubas and timpani calling out the heartbeat of Earth. Catching glimpses of the frogs took patience and a light step on the banks, but I managed after several tries to capture some images on my camera.

My obsession with the frogs turned to love. I confessed to Tom, who urged me not to kiss one, lest it turn into a prince. No chance, I said. I'm not interested in princes. I loved the frogs. I loved that they made me stop and listen, held in rapture long enough to realize the value of seeing nature not just as a problem to fix, but where we can all find wonder and belonging.

An essayist's words came to mind. She wrote about the moment she realized her own body was a piece of divine nature entrusted to her care, and how that opens the heart to caring for our fellow humans and other creatures. In the protests, we were combining all our voices to decry the violence committed against those we are entrusted to cherish. Like the bullfrog chorus, all the individual voices in the protests—black, brown and white, young and old—converged into a force of wonder and inspiration. There is much about the human world that needs fixing. Stopping to name the marvels of humanity is perhaps the best way to find motivation for the task.

Happenstance brought Angie and me to Wadsworth Falls State Park on that lavish June afternoon. It turned into a chance encounter with grace.

Friends since childhood, we decided to meet at the park for a hike because it was near where her daughter would be taking a four-hour test for her nursing license. Angie and Nora had just driven from their home in New Jersey through the heart of the New York City megalopolis, so time outdoors would be a welcome interlude before the return trip.

After our parking lot reunion with pandemic-style air hugs, we found the well-worn trail through the woods to the waterfall. Along the way, we chatted about our families and jobs, and about the eruption of protests since the George Floyd killing. The rush of anger and resolve from the Black Lives Matter march I had joined with my husband two days earlier was still fresh in my mind. The protest Angie tried to join was rained out, but she was determined to find another and had been communicating with her boss about diversifying their workplace.

We grew up together in Dover, N.J., attending public schools there with a broad mix of Hispanic, African American and white kids like ourselves. I would be naïve to say racial tensions never flared, but I honestly don't remember any. "Live and let live," seemed the unspoken motto. Peers from the whiter, wealthier towns around us looked down on Dover, but thanks to one straight-talking high school history teacher, my friends and I knew Dover had something rich and rare in its diversity. Even if we didn't fully appreciate it then, the years since have only intensified that realization. Today, Angie and I both still live in diverse communities and enjoy longtime friendships with people of all colors.

But neither of us were feeling too comfortable with ourselves since current events blared "white privilege" alongside "I can't breathe." What's an effective way to acknowledge all this pain and injustice, then take meaningful concrete action? Simply cogitating on what's wrong, I told her, seemed like a waste of time, more like avoidance than responsibility. I needed to find how to play my part. She agreed.

Then the trail ended at a paved road. Where was the waterfall? We saw some arrows pointing the way. It took us across a grassy field, then down some rustic wooden stairs.

There it was. Magnificently tumbling off the rock cliff into sparkling pools below, the waterfall held a gathered congregation of humanity in thrall. Afternoon sun rays streamed through the canopy. Angie and I found a spot along the banks near three young African American men, who smiled and chatted as one waded in the water. On the other side a mom spoke to her daughter in Spanish. Children splashed in the pools. Others drenched themselves directly beneath the waterfall. I've had many precious experiences in nature over the years, but never in the midst of so much diversity. The mix looked just like Dover.

What were we witnessing but God's grace? I turned to Angie, tearful. This is so beautiful, I told her, just to see people playing, hear them laughing, receiving the gifts of nature. After so many days of turmoil, we could all just soak in the wonder of living for a few moments together here. It's the reason to keep reaching for more, for better.

A few days later, we exchanged emails. Angie had been to a protest and initiated a diversity hiring initiative at work. I had gotten the OK from my boss to devote the next issue of the magazine I edit to issues of diversity in the sciences, and environmental racism. It was just a small start, but it felt good. The waterfall of God's grace had led the way.

Awaken your long-slumbering six-year-old with a few hours at the beach. The sand, sweat, salt and surf stir the senses back to that little person you once were, so open to the full sensory overload of the seashore. The briny smell, the cawing gulls, the hot gritty grains between your toes, the seaweed taste on your lips can bring you back to your young animal self, closer to the Earth and other creatures in body and mind.

A child digging at the edge of the tide is the most intent of all builders. Follow that lead. Immerse yourself in the moment—this moment before the next wave washes it away.

Then drift off to sleep in the midday sun. Float on a current of memory mixed with the giggling of the children running around the next blanket over. When you wake, plunge into the sea. Your six-year-old-self is still alive and well within.

Starlight

50

Twilight chiseled the silhouette of the American basswood tree into a soft-shouldered hilltop that seemed to hold the Big Dipper as it emerged from the darkening sky. Its branches thick with heart-shaped leaves in the fullness of summer, the tree grew some 30 feet tall a short walk from the campfire. Whenever I looked up from the dancing flames, my gaze was drawn to that shapely rooted presence and then upward to the stars and wispy clouds.

It was the second night of our short stay in the campground at Hammonassett Beach State Park. The day had been long and full, the time stretched with the joys of true leisure. There was a meetup with Roxanne on the beach, a dip in the sea and an encounter with a horseshoe crab sweeping its ancient frame through the shallow water for us to admire. There was time to meander through marsh trails, tiptoe close to bunnies and egrets and nap in the shade. Before sunset came a swim with Tom then a simple and satisfying meal cooked over a wood fire. The stars gave the grand finale.

When had I last looked at the night sky—really looked? The enveloping dark revealed a truth so easy for us humans to forget as we scurry and worry in our everyday existence. There are too many stars to count, the universe too vast to comprehend, and our lives are but a blink in the expanse of the infinite. Reminded of the great mystery, I am humbled and awestruck. Starlight from millions of miles away sent earthward millions of years ago now reaches my eye, stirs my emotions. This is wonder.

Eroded Boulder House in Hovenweep National Monument in Utah is a most curious dwelling. Created by ancient Pueblo people sometime around 1200 AD, it sits within a canyon rimmed by the ruins of brick towers and castles that remain from an ancient village. Each structure is fascinating in its own way, but Eroded Boulder House stands out as the most unique. A huge rock sitting exposed on a flat space of dry earth had been hollowed out, presumably first by forces of nature and then carved deeper by human hands. The top of the boulder forms the roof. Inside, part of a brick wall remains. When I saw it a few summers ago, I tried imagining what the lives of the former occupants were like.

This summer, other kinds of shelters have caught my attention. Kayaking on Eagleville Dam into the Willimantic River one August day, my husband Tom and I spotted a muskrat lodge on the shore. The dome of sticks and mud reminded me of a small tent I had spotted in a neighbor's front yard a day earlier. Walking past I saw the sides bulge and heard children inside laughing. A thin sheet of nylon and a few poles had transformed a space on the grass into a private hive for play. The muskrat, those children and all of us share a common instinct, for a womb of one's own to encapsulate a piece of the open Earth. Defining a space as ours, even for an afternoon on a beach blanket, signifies that we belong there for this present moment. Only the most ardent nomads resist this urge.

Earlier in the summer after the pandemic upended everyone's vacation plans, Tom and I found ourselves driven to seek out a new kind of shelter. Quite unexpectedly, we purchased a small camper so we could safely travel and find the refreshment we both needed. In Vermont and Maine, we parked our little camper and called patches of woods our home for a few days, while we explored a fog forest, mountain streams and seacoast islands. For a time we belonged to other places, where the cares of work and tumultuous current events could be suspended. We could breathe deep and fall in love with life and nature anew. Making shelter and re-creating in a new place connected us to another part of this planet, renewing our capacity to care about it all.

Autumn

Lookout Point

Woodland Loop

Stone Walls

Blue Moon

November Marsh

Sat. Oct 10, 2020 Incarnation Center; Ivoryton, CT. Looking up at Look-Out Point

For a falcon, this is the typical viewpoint, perched or hovering above the rest of the Earth. Hiking the trail to Lookout Point took less than an hour and some moderate leg muscle, since the cliff rises just 400 feet above Bushy Hill Lake at Incarnation Center. Yet this bare rock shoulder offered a full measure of uplift in the fresh perspective to be found there.

As Roxanne and I started on the red trail around the pond that bright, warm October morning, gusts whooshed through branches still thick with leaves, crickets clicked and birds chirped. But the gold- and scarlet-tinged woods were otherwise quiet. Then, as we rounded the north end of the pond, we heard distant voices—children's voices. Summer sleepover camps hadn't happened here since before the pandemic, so these sounds seemed otherworldly, like echoes from the past seeping through an unseen portal into the present.

When we reached Lookout Point, we saw the source. Across the lake, one of the docks bobbed under the weight of eight or 10 boys in bathing suits. One dashed off the end, curled himself into a ball in the air and hit the water with a grand splash. Another followed. Laughter flew aloft on the wind. Later, we passed them on one of the trails with their teacher. Some wore T-shirts for a boys choir school, and later we heard their angelic voices from one of the camp buildings. Live group singing! We had all been deprived of this most ancient form of human music by the pandemic. Now it sounded like part of some happy dream.

That afternoon, I returned to Lookout Point by myself. I resolved to linger there, heed the literal meaning of the place name and look out again. This time, there were no laughing, splashing boys to see from afar. My attention turned to the wind, moving the limbs of a tall oak to dance and sway like a falcon catching an updraft. It rippled the surface of the lake. The wind was touching me, too, tossing my hair around, brushing my cheeks, moving across all of me and maybe even through me.

At Lookout Point that day, I had witnessed a scene of simple childhood joy and then found my own simple joy in watching the wind. "We don't see things as they are, we see them as we are," the writer Anais Nin once said. Perhaps she is right. But from the vantage at Lookout Point, I became someone with eyes and heart opened a bit wider to beauty.

Nine months ago we had last pressed our feet to the rocks, roots and marl of the trails at Incarnation Center. Then, the world was a different place, not yet chastened by the COVID pandemic now still raging into the fall. By returning here, Roxanne and I could to bring our project full circle, maybe find a way to connect pre- and post-pandemic phases of existence I could scarcely believe had happened in the same year.

We set out that morning on the trail around Bushy Hill Lake, starting the opposite way from last time. Back in February, we had only done the southern half of this trail. Then, we found it rich in treasures— needle ice, strong winter shadows, docks and a rope swing over the water to remind us of summer delights. Completing the whole loop now felt like a heeding a natural impulse.

We came to a tree adorned with shapely shelves of fungus, cream and golden brown against the ash- colored bark. Checking a nature guide later, images of a species called artist's bracket or bear bread seemed to match what we saw. Artful though it looked, the fungus signaled the tree's decay. Farther along, several large fallen trees forced us to detour off the trail for short stretches. The recent wind storms that had felled power lines in many communities came to mind. In the fungus and blowdown, the forest offered reminders that the perpetual state of transition for all life can be swift or gradual. Or, as with the pandemic, it can be both simultaneously.

By lunchtime we ended up back where we started. Or did we? Time had passed, the Earth had turned, and the warm smells and colors of the autumn woods had massaged our pandemic-weary souls. Taking time for beauty and wonder may be the best coping strategy of all.

Cuff Candol, Sarah Cyrus, Joseph Pumham and Prentiss Crosley once lived there. They and their sons and daughters built many of the stone walls, foundations and charcoal pits today's hikers pass along the trails at Hartman Park.

These were people of Native American and African American descent, many of them enslaved by European settlers before they broke free and joined the community that lumbered, farmed and hunted this piece of ground in the 18th and 19th centuries. Before that, these woods were a favorite place for the Nehantic tribe to find game. They would regularly burn the understory to open the views, leaving many old growth trees white settlers later cleared to supply the British naval fleet that came to dominate the seas.

A sign at the threshold of Hartman Park tells this story, names some of those who once called this home. It's an effort at land acknowledgement, a practice meant to honor the indigenous communities that lived on and cared for the places our towns, homes and parks now occupy. We need more reminders like this. Succumbing to collective amnesia about the past seems all too easy in this chaotic, distracted modern age.

At another favorite hiking spot, stone walls line both sides of the main trail. Many old cart roads throughout New England that have become hiking paths are similarly appointed. Whether they were the work of Native Americans or Colonial settlers, these structures built from the rock mountains unloaded by the glaciers now appear part of the natural landscape. After centuries of settling, they have become the favorite adopted homes of chipmunks and snakes, man-made alterations that became part of the forest habitat.

What will this era leave behind? Will any of it be incorporated into nature, like the stone walls? Maybe this is something to strive for, in our personal and collective actions—creations that don't scar the landscape, but instead age gracefully into it.

Blue Moon

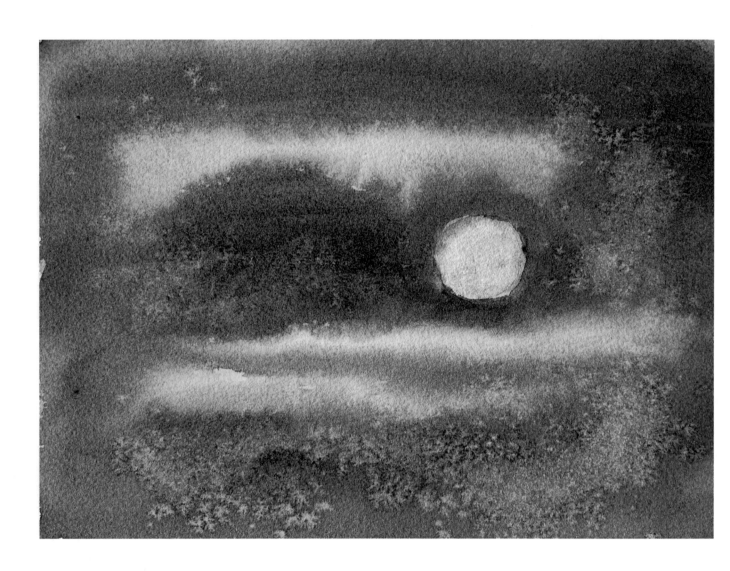

On Halloween night, the glow of the blue moon backlit the tawny clouds. Though 236,855 miles away, that big boyish visage seemed much closer, playing hide-and-seek as it rose out of the horizon until it reached the open sky. It had earned the special name for being the second full moon in the same month, a rarity meriting our attention. Making plans with my husband and some friends to watch the blue moon rise felt like a spiritual act, a way of remembering ourselves as small parts of something still unfathomable.

Camped on a quiet beach for the pageant, we recalled songs about the moon and chatted about life, but mostly just admired the perfect yellow orb that briefly took our minds off the cares of this Earth. Geologists say the moon was once a part of the Earth, broken free in chunks when a planet struck, then spun into this enchanting sphere that wields power over the tides and, some say, sometimes our psyches.

Three weeks later, I stopped to admire the moon again. This time, it was in the waxing crescent phase, just after the new moon. Seeing it on an early evening walk just after sunset, the silver sliver looked like a giant celestial comma, punctuating the night sky with a subtle message. Pause. Take a breath. Lift your eyes.

I had started the walk feeling weary from the tedious tasks and frustrations of the workday. In the cool night air and the open sky, that slip of the moon reminded me again how to free myself from the envelope of my own ego. Step away from yourself and take stock of the grand scheme of things.

November Marsh

Frost-sheathed grass sparkled and delicate vapor clouds floated off the marsh as the early morning sun pierced the sky over Barn Island Wildlife Management Area. Along the trail, the brackish pools in the marsh appeared still, yet distinct gurgling sounds filled the quiet to tell a different story.

With the high tide, salt water from the Atlantic gushed in, swirling into whirlpools as it funneled into the culverts that would carry it to the far upper reaches of this land-sea transition zone. A section of stone wall visible in the flooded high marsh memorialized the changes past and coming more rapidly to places like this at the sea's edge.

For the farmer who built that wall in some former century, this had been land dry enough for hay crops and grazing cows. The rising sea had claimed it decades ago and keeps spreading farther and faster as the planet warms. Climate change can and should be slowed but can't be stopped altogether. Instead of fighting or denying our vulnerability to Earth's forces, can we learn to accommodate them? Can we step back from the shore with our roads and buildings, not as an act of defeat but as a part of realizing a vision of a better future for nature and humans alike?

Sometimes loving the beauty and solace of the outdoors comes some sadness. It can feel like spending time with an old beloved soul, ever conscious of her mortality. Yet we don't stop caring, we don't give up on their life. Maybe nature asks the same of us.

Acknowledgements

We have many people to thank for their support and encouragement for this project. First, much gratitude goes to the Incarnation Center for giving us a place to start and end our project, the bookends that helped us frame our work.

Personal thanks from Judy: to my husband Tom for his love and wisdom, to my lifelong friends Linda Huff-Paul for her sensitive but incisive editing, and Angela D'Agostino for her insightful comments; Larry Tye, Helen Rozwadowski and Claudia Weicker for their generous endorsements; Christine Woodside for her friendship, supportive response to the early drafts and beautiful Foreword; New London Landmarks Executive Director Laura Natusch for encouraging us to submit this to New London Librarium; and to Glenn Cheney for his professional and respectful handling of our work. And of course much love and gratitude go to Roxanne for being my friend and creative partner.

Personal thanks from Roxanne: Thank you to Judy for suggesting this book several years ago. When the pandemic hit, we knew this was the right time to work on this. Thanks to my husband Ron for always supporting and encouraging my art business endeavors. Much gratitude to both my Monday Writers and Illustrators groups for their encouragement, and my Friday night study buddies across the US and Canada with "Making Art Work." We are stronger together than we are alone.

The Illustrations

Places Mentioned in Essays:

- Incarnation Center, 235 Bushy Hill Road, Deep River, CT www.incarnationcenter.org
- Hartman Park, 122 Gungy Road, Lyme, CT www.lymelandtrust.org
- Barn Island Wildlife Management Area, 249 Palmer Neck Road, Pawcatuck, CT https:/ /portal.ct.gov/-/media/DEEP/stateparks/maps/BarnIslandTrail2012pdf.pdf

State Parks:

- Bluff Point State Park, Depot Road, Groton, CT
- Hammonasset Beach State Park, 1288 Boston Post Road, Madison, CT
- Harkness Memorial State Park, 275 Great Neck Road, Waterford, CT
- Wadsworth Falls State Park, 721 Wadsworth St., Middletown, CT

  Link to information about CT State Parks:

  https://portal.ct.gov/DEEP/State-Parks/Listing-of-State-Parks

Judy Benson

Judy Benson has been the communications coordinator at Connecticut Sea Grant and editor of its award-winning biannual magazine *Wrack Lines* since 2017. Before that she worked as a reporter and editor at several Connecticut newspapers, concluding her daily journalism career as the health and environment reporter at *The Day* of New London. She earned both her bachelor's degree in journalism and a Master of Science in natural resources from the University of Connecticut. In addition to writing articles for *Wrack Lines*, her creative non-fiction essays and opinion pieces have been published in *Appalachia*, Connecticut Woodlands, Connecticut Hearst newspapers, *The Connecticut Mirror* and *The Day*. She lives with her husband in southeastern Connecticut, a part of the world they love for its many public open spaces, shoreline and easy access to great camping spots throughout New England.

Roxanne Steed

Roxanne Steed is a painter of well-loved places, a traveler, gardener, nature lover and teacher. She began painting in her younger years, trying out watercolors, pastels, oil and acrylics and savoring them all. Throughout her years as a Navy wife, she found opportunities for great training in each of the many places she and her family lived. Formal study at the Lyme Academy College of Fine Arts in Old Lyme, CT; The Art League School in Alexandria, VA; and Watts Atelier in Encinitas, CA, gave her a classical foundation. Roxanne focused on oil painting for 20 years before being drawn back to the natural beauty of watercolors in 2013. She teaches in that medium and her biggest thrill is watching her students discover and grow their love of painting. While her home, studio and main teaching venue is in southeastern Connecticut, she also leads artist workshops in the U.S. and abroad.

Christine Woodside

Christine Woodside is a Connecticut-based writer and author of *Libertarians on the Prairie: Laura Ingalls Wilder, Rose Wilder Lane and the Making of Little House Books*. She edits the journal *Appalachia* and is at work on a wilderness memoir, *The Long Way Home*, which Appalachian Mountain Club Books will publish in 2023.

She sometimes leads nature-writing workshops and loves teaching undergraduates journalism history. Visit her at chriswoodside.com.

New London Librarium

New London Librarium is a literary press in Hanover, Conn. It specializes in books that merit publication but are unlikely to achieve the sales expected by larger publishers. NLL offers series on Catholic issues, environmental issues, Brazil, history, art, and general interest. For more information, see NLLibrarium.com.

Made in United States
North Haven, CT
06 November 2021